Dak Prescott: The Inspiring Story of One of Football's Top Quarterbacks

An Unauthorized Biography

By: Clayton Geoffreys

Table of Contents

Foreword

Once just a backup quarterback, Dak Prescott became the Dallas Cowboys' starting quarterback when Tony Romo became injured in preseason. Prescott rose to the occasion, helping his team secure the top seed in their conference while also setting several rookie quarterback records. That year, Prescott was also named the NFL Offensive Rookie of the Year and a Pro Bowler. In just his fifth season at the time of this writing, the future is bright for Dak Prescott. The Cowboys have already placed the franchise tag on Prescott in 2020. Dak suffered a season-ending injury in October 2020; however, he should still have many years left of dominance as a quarterback in the NFL. Thank you for purchasing *Dak Prescott: The Inspiring Story of One of Football's Top Quarterbacks*. In this unauthorized biography, we will learn Dak Prescott's incredible life story and impact on the game of football. Hope you enjoy and if you do, please do not forget to leave a review!

Also, check out my website at claytongeoffreys.com to join my exclusive list where I let you know about my latest books. To thank you for your purchase, you can go to my site to download a free copy of *33 Life Lessons: Success Principles, Career Advice & Habits of Successful People.* In the book, you'll learn from some of the greatest thought leaders of different industries on what it takes to become successful and how to live a great life.

Cheers,

Clayton Geoffreys

Visit me at www.claytongeoffreys.com

Introduction

When Dak Prescott was drafted in the fourth round of the 2016 NFL Draft by the Dallas Cowboys, the expectation was that he would battle with Mark Sanchez for the backup quarterback role behind Tony Romo. But when Romo went down with a broken bone in his back that cost him the season and led to his retirement, Prescott was thrust into the starting role.

Four years later, he's not only still there, but he is also one of the most successful quarterbacks in the league. In four seasons, he has thrown for over 3,000 yards four times and 4,000 yards once. His 98 touchdowns rank among the leaders for most touchdowns thrown since 2016.

Prescott has become one of the best dual-threat quarterbacks in the NFL. He is the only quarterback in history to throw for 20 or more touchdowns while rushing for five or more touchdowns in each of his first three seasons. He was the 2016 NFL Rookie of the Year winner, helping lead his team to the playoffs, and has been to the Pro Bowl twice in his four-year career, including as a rookie.[i]

As a college quarterback at Mississippi State University, Prescott helped make Dan Mullen's offense one of the best in the country. He was named to the All-SEC First Team twice and helped lead his team to a 10-3 record and their first-ever Orange Bowl appearance in 2014.[i] He is the all-time leader in career touchdowns and single-game touchdowns at MSU.

Prescott's story goes far beyond football, however. Not many know the tale of how he was able to become the starting quarterback for America's team. Off the field, Prescott is a class act and a role model for all young athletes to emulate. Prescott doesn't just exemplify confidence, leadership, and knowledge, he shows genuine concern for others, treats others with respect, demonstrates humility, and accepts mistakes when he makes them and tries to correct them. Those who have played with Prescott have called him a natural-born leader. It is these kinds of traits that make him one of the most admired athletes in the game.

Prescott's rise into the spotlight is a great underdog story. He was never even talked about in 2016 during the NFL Draft. People doubted him as a quarterback and thought he would make a better tight end or wide receiver than a quarterback, given his size and ability to run. Prescott used those doubts as his motivation. He worked extremely hard and believed in himself, knowing that he had the potential to not just prove to others that he could make it to the top, but to prove it to himself as well.

But while Prescott dealt with low expectations when he came into NFL, he was the subject of high expectations in high school and college. Prescott grew up in the South, where football dominates and you have the opportunity to play against some of the best athletes in the country. He went to Haughton High

School in Louisiana and helped lead his team to a state title. He credits a lot of his success to his mother, with whom he is extremely close. She helped inspire him and his brothers. She loved football growing up and even had a football tattooed on her arm. Her dream was for one of her sons to make it as a professional. She would watch her sons play in the backyard with the neighbors and always knew Dak had the ability to be great. One of Prescott's driving forces was to make her dream a reality. While some people were surprised by his success, she never was. She knew he had it in him.

Family means so much to Dak. He frequently talks about how important it is in life and to lean on them during tough times. That camaraderie with his family has helped him to build healthy relationships with his new family on the football field. You could say he has treated his coaches like his mother—giving them the respect they deserve and using their words as lessons to get better on the field, just like he used his mother's lessons to get better in life. All of his coaches have said Prescott demonstrated the leadership you would want out of a player, especially a quarterback. He gives his all in everything he does and will do whatever it takes to succeed.[ii]

"The biggest thing with Dak is his work ethic," former Mississippi State and former Florida Gators coach Dan Mullen said. "He is always trying to get himself better, whether it be how fast he's making his reads and his decision-making when things break down."[iii]

That is what you want in a great quarterback: someone who keeps trying to improve themselves and creates new goals when they reach their current ones. The best in the world never accept the status quo; rather, they push for new heights. According to Mullen, that's Prescott. He's always trying to get to that next level. Prescott has said that he is hard on himself and that he is his own biggest critic. That is the way most great athletes are.

After high school, Prescott had the opportunity to go to LSU, who had offered him a scholarship to play football there. But Prescott was impressed with Mullen and wanted to go somewhere where he could start a new tradition and help a struggling team rise that had not achieved the same kind of storied success that LSU had already enjoyed. He decided that Mississippi State was the perfect place for him to be a leader and help the team grow. And he was absolutely right—Dak indeed helped put MSU on the map. Under his leadership, the Bulldogs were ranked number one in the nation for the very first time in history and the school experienced a huge boost in enrollments as well.

Prescott was also an outstanding student growing up, not just a great athlete. While helping Mississippi State achieve new heights as a starting quarterback, he was also earning straight 'A's in the classroom and made it to the All-SEC Academic Honor Roll in 2013. Dak believed in the importance of staying focused on academics. To him, that was just as critical, if not more critical, than what you did on the football field. Getting an education is something that should always be a priority and never be taken for granted, no matter how your future may pan out as an athlete.[ii] Sooner or later, you are going to need it. Dak knew, although many young aspiring athletes, unfortunately, do not realize it, that your academic education benefits your athletic performance, too.

"I am a smarter person because I stayed in school," Prescott said. "And that's helped make me a better football player, too."[iv]

One of Prescott's biggest dreams was to be the quarterback of the Dallas Cowboys. His dad was a huge fan and Prescott loved the team, too. But Dak has been working hard to realize another dream as well. He has said that, while he wants to make a difference *on* the field, making a difference *off* the field has been an even bigger goal. Dak has been very active in charity work and most notably has helped boys and girls all across the country to have a better life. He has teamed up with the Marshall Boys and Girls Club, participating in events, making appearances, donating items, and giving financially to them as well as other organizations.

Prescott is a true hero and his story is both exciting and inspirational. He is someone that many young athletes aspire to be like, and someone to watch, as rarely have we seen such a unique and exceptional talent on the football field.

Let us explore how Dak Prescott got to where he is today.

Chapter 1: Early Childhood

Rayne Dakota Prescott, the youngest of three boys, was born on July 29, 1993, in Sulphur, Louisiana. As a toddler, he was called Rayne, but by school age, he began going by his middle name Dakota, and then finally by just "Dak." He actually got his middle name from one of three bulls, "Dakota Duke," on the cartoon show, *Wild West C.O.W. Boys of Moo Mesa*.[ix]

His parents, Nathaniel and Peggy Prescott, both played very different roles in his life. Dak was of mixed ethnicity, with his father being black and his mother, white. The couple divorced when Dak was very young. Although Nathaniel, known as Nat, has still been there for him throughout his life, it was his mother who raised him.[v]

Dak's mother played the biggest role in his life growing up. As a single mother, she pushed him to always get better in everything he did and he has followed that credo throughout his life. When Dak was little, his mom would bring him out to their backyard with her two other boys and let them play football while she sat and watched them play. Luckily, they had some space behind their home. The "football field" was not big, certainly not your typical 100-yard space, but Dak said it was a full field to *them*. About 30 or 40 yards in length and width, Dak, his brothers, and his friends would make that small space their home field. Over time, more boys would even come and join them. It may not have been much, but it was football for them.[xxix]

Peggy was always a huge football fan, long before any of her children showed any aptitude for the game. She had the number three and a football tattooed on her arm. The number representing her three boys that meant more than anything to her.

Dak worshipped his mother. He called his relationship with her "crazy close." In fact, as close as he and his brothers were growing up, his mom was always that little bit more special to him.[vi]

"I love my brothers to death, but my mom was something that no one could ever mimic that relationship," Prescott said. "My brothers were my good friends; they were my best friends. But they weren't my best-est of friends."[vi]

It really is a great story when you can point to your mom or your dad as your inspiration in life. Dak was so close to his mom as a little boy, they even shared the same room together—even, at times, by choice. When his brothers went away to college and Dak was still in the sixth grade and could have moved into one of their rooms, he chose to stay with his mom and still share that room.

Peggy never coddled him, however. She pushed Dak hard as a child. Whenever Dak was nervous about playing football or being picked on by kids because of his mixed race, his mom gave him words of encouragement.

"She wasn't really comforting," Prescott said. "She was telling me, 'You're either going to be tough or you're going to stay inside and sit with me. You're going to be tough and go out there and hang with them.'"[vi]

Dak struggled a bit to get along with other kids and was sometimes picked on as a child because of racial prejudice. Dak was a half-black kid growing up in an all-white town and some of the local kids gave him a hard time. Haughton, Louisiana was not a "kind" town back then. While some great athletes are fortunate enough to grow up in the perfect environment, for Dak it was the opposite. He grew up in a trailer park and his family struggled with poverty. Many times, his grandparents had to help his mother financially, who was often struggling to make ends meet as she worked the graveyard shift at a truck stop.

Along with his mother, his grandparents played an important, comforting, and supportive role in his life. He loved going over to their house and spending time with them. His grandfather was a high school principal and gave him a lot of great words of advice on how to handle the racial criticism he was experiencing. This helped Dak a lot to transition and become a more mature person.

Still, things were not easy for Dak. Growing up in a trailer park, there were times they were so financially strapped that his mother could not even pay the electric bill, at which times they would have to go to the cheapest motel they could find nearby. His mother worked as hard as she possibly could, however, picking up as many hours as her work would allow, to make sure her sons could experience a better future. Eventually, she became the manager at a truck stop in Haughton to help pick up a little more income.

In an interview with journalist Graham Bensinger in September 2020, Prescott discussed how difficult his childhood was. Prescott said his mother did whatever it took for her family to survive. For Peggy, it was hard, but for Dak and his brothers, it was sometimes actually fun. They went swimming at the motel and knew that everything would be okay because they had a mother who would fight to make sure they were okay. Amazingly, and even more to Peggy's credit, the brothers had no idea of the overwhelming stress the family was enduring at the time.[xxix]

"My mom did such a great job at masking the adversity and the struggle," Dak said. "Me and my brothers were so young, we didn't realize what was going on. We just thought we were on vacation at a motel. As we got older, we realized what she was doing."[xxix]

Prescott's home was not exactly what you would see on Mansion Row. There was no 50-inch high definition television. They had a small TV that sat on top of another broken television, which in turn sat on top of a box that acted as a stand, complete with antennas that had foil on them to help try to produce a picture. There was no cable, just a couple of channels, which was enough for the family to watch *Survivor* or football games on the weekends. Meanwhile, Peggy was doing whatever she could to make things work.[xxix]

Dak's father worked for the Louisiana oil fields much of his life before then getting a job as a commercial driver and working for an Austin city bus company. It is unknown how much Dak saw his father when he was younger, although he would play a bigger role in his life later on. When he got older, his father moved closer to Dak when he became a member of the Dallas Cowboys. But during those earlier trying days, he was on his own trying to make his own living, struggling to survive. "Nat" was going from job to job, city to city, and fighting his own battles.

Dak said those days in the trailer park changed him and made him who he was. He said it is why he acts so nice towards people and always wants to help people out, knowing the struggles that they could be going through.

"I'm so proud of where I lived and got to experience what I went through," Dak said. "I never saw it as a struggle. If I did, it would discredit my mom and my brothers. If I didn't go through what I went through, I wouldn't be the person I am today."

Sometimes we take for granted our lives. We have our own trivial problems where we complain about the little things, such as having no internet for an hour or having our phone die. We do not realize that there are people going through so much worse. Good people who have uncertain futures and are fighting to survive life, making the best out of their situations. Dak's family would laugh at anyone who complained about their air conditioning not working for a day. They had to deal with not having air conditioning, sometimes for a whole month, and in the sweltering Louisiana 100-degree heat.[xxix]

When you combine those financial challenges with the moments of racial bullying that Dak faced, it was not easy times, but you would not know it by looking at Dak. Those that knew him best said he never let it get to him much of the time, and when it did bother him, he confronted it. Dak became strong because of his childhood experiences. Every day's goal was to simply get through the day, and when tomorrow came, you dealt with it then.

Dak said he wishes more people could experience what he went through growing up because it would mature them, especially in a world today where people complain about such little, inconsequential things. He calls it the best experience of his life and one that grew his respect for his mom even more.

Dak and his brothers became closer because of those days while their mom worked. But it did not come without its share of hazing and teasing. As the younger brother, Dak got the classic "little brother" treatment. When he and his brothers were asked during an interview on Facebook what his favorite food memory was as a child, Dak said it was the eating contests he had with them. They were always so competitive, trying to top the other. "When you're a little brother, you try a lot of things," Dak said. "They just put stuff together and you eat it."[xl]

Dak's brothers said some of the stuff they ate were some of the grossest things, but that was the fun they had when they were not playing football. They spent a lot of time together because of the situation they were in, and it was his brothers' football skills that motivated Dak to also want to play and be even better than them.

The family was competitive. They always tried to top each other one way or the other, whether it was who could eat Oreo cookies the fastest or who could throw the football the furthest. "Sometimes it was to see who could take the most pain," Dak said. That meant playing games with pencils and knuckles or throwing phones on each other's ribs to see who could take it. In their games with food, it was about who could eat the grossest things. They were always trying to beat each other.[xli]

Dak said he never forgot the one and only time he ever complained to his mother about being harassed by others. "She said, 'If you don't want to play with the big dogs, then just sit on the porch.' When she said that, I said I don't care what it takes, I'm going to go out there. They can beat me up, they can make me cry, but I'm going to come back and I'm going to come back every single time."[xli]

Mothers are known for a lot of things, but Dak will always remember his mother for making him tougher. It was not until later on in life when they found out the stress she was under. At times, Peggy was concerned that the government was going to come in and take her kids away because of her financial struggles and ability to make enough money to support them. Luckily, they also had grandparents who were willing to help out in any way and offered a safe haven if the children ever needed it.[xli]

Dak's brothers were good at sports and while Dak was in the seventh grade, he would go to see his older brothers play on the Haughton high school team. But the coaches had their eye on young Dak even while coaching his brothers. They had seen him play in middle school and knew he had special skills. As a seventh-grader, Dak was strong and athletic and had an impressive arm. When Haughton coach Rodney Guin saw Dak, the first thing he noticed about him was his competitive spirit. "It didn't matter if he was playing basketball or tug-of-war. He wanted to win," Guin said.[viii]

Quarterback was not Prescott's initial position. While he had a strong arm and showed his gunslinger skills off in backyard games behind their home, his youth coach had him playing linebacker and running back. Part of the reason for that was his size, but also because the coach's son was the team's quarterback. It was also thought that, because both his brothers played on the offensive and defensive line on the high school team, Dak would wind up there, too. But during his sixth year of recreational ball, that head coach got an insurance job and had to leave the team. The new coach instantly put Prescott in at quarterback and that's where he stayed.[x]

"When I got into high school," Prescott said, "many years before that, the coaches that were coaching my brothers, the offensive coordinator, I love him to death and he's a great friend of mine–for years he said 'he won't be a quarterback. He won't be the quarterback of this team.' Sure enough, I get to high school, catch a little growth spurt and I started playing quarterback and throwing the ball well. By my sophomore year, there was no doubt."[x]

Most great players do not start at the position that they become famous for. Patrick Mahomes, who did not throw a football in a game until his sophomore year in high school, started out as a cornerback. Mike Trout was a shortstop. Babe Ruth a pitcher. Kyler Murray was supposed to be a baseball player. Ichiro Suzuki, a pitcher. There is always something that seems to draw them to the position they would one day become famous for.

Prescott's competitive spirit could be attributed to his brothers and his mother. Not only did his mother push him, but growing up as the youngest of three boys, he was teased a lot and he always wanted to get back at his brothers by beating them in football or basketball or whatever sport they played. The fire always burned inside of him and he brought it out more and more as he got older.

Dak credits his brother Jace for becoming a quarterback. Jace, the middle brother of the three, sadly passed away at 31-years-old, when Prescott was already a member of the Cowboys. As a boy, Jace was very close to Dak and helped build the competitive spirit inside him. He helped him become a better football player, along with being a better quarterback. When Jace passed away, Dak said that Jace had played a huge role in him making it as a professional.[viii]

People who knew Dak best as a child described him as a very outgoing, talkative person. "He could talk the horns off a Billy goat as a little boy," his cousin Pam Ebarb said. His family knew him as Dakota. His cousin Pam, though, also described Dakota as the "sweetest boy I ever knew" and said you could not help but not get along with him. He was always cheerful and also loved to always look good, having an appreciation for fashion.[ix] It is amazing that despite all he went through as a child, he still kept a positive attitude in everything he did and, as his family and friends described him, always had a smile on his face. Times were tough, but you could not tell it by looking at Dak.[ix]

As Dak prepared to enter high school, his life was beginning to round into form. He was getting good grades in school and the racial prejudice he had experienced earlier on in his life was subsiding. He was making more friends and was discovering a passion in his life: football. His mother was also making more money and was pushing him to become better at the game he was loving. Prescott was about to discover over the next four years just how much football would play a role in his future life.

Chapter 2: High School Career

The Fantastic Five

They called them "The Fantastic Five" and they all had their nicknames. Prescott, the quarterback, was known in his group as Superman. Trent Jacobs, who would become the kid that Prescott roped many of his great passes to, was Spiderman. Slot receiver Jordan Craft was blessed with great speed and was called Flash. The last two receivers were Damon Gladney, known as Mr. Fantastic, and Marlon Seets, who was Mr. Incredible.[vii]

These were not just the guys that Dak would play football with in high school; they were the four boys that Dak shared a close bond with for most of his life. Dak's mother was like *their* mother, too. They always called her "Miss Peggy." The boys played in the backyard with Dak and his brothers and hung out together constantly. The boys also always went out trick-or-treating together on Halloween and used to play pranks on each other, particularly Prescott. They loved messing with Dak and continued to do so in high school.

"We'd hide his cleats before practice just so we could see him freak out," Gladney said. "It was hilarious. It got to the point where, 'Oh, I hadn't messed with Dak this week. It's getting close to game day and I have to do something.'"[vii]

While it was all in fun and they loved him, his friends enjoyed messing with him because he was "The Golden Boy." They knew from day one that he would be going on to greater things because he was so talented. That made it easier to pick on him. "The coaches, though, made sure it didn't happen too often," Gladney said.[vii]

The Fantastic Five teased him, but they also had a massive amount of respect for him. Jacobs said he had more passion for the game than anyone they knew. He proved it furthermore in high school, which included a district title game in his senior year where he led his team back and ran a one-yard quarterback sneak to win the championship, despite playing with a sprained MCL.[vii]

When Dak began high school football, there were a lot of expectations for him after what coaches had seen from him previously. He not only had great size for a young boy, but he also had an incredible arm and the ability to make plays with his legs, something that would carry with him all throughout his career. Glenn Benton, a graduate from the school in the 1960s, always went to their games and reminisced about how good Dak and his brothers were when he watched them.

"One of the coaches pulled me aside and said, 'You think his brothers are good? Wait until (Dak) comes around,'" Benton said. "Those coaches were licking their lips when he was in the seventh grade."[ix]

Sometimes that is not always the best thing, though. Having such lofty expectations placed on you when you are so young puts a lot of pressure on you. It would have gotten to a lot of guys, but Dak's adversity early in life helped in high school. Going through such tough times as a child and having a mother who perpetually pushed him the way she did had made him tough and resilient. His mom and others always called him a bull, not just because of his size, but because of his toughness.

His coaches were impressed by him. "He wasn't a real loud guy," Guin, his high school coach, said. "He wasn't the guy who screamed and got in your face. He was someone who led by example–and that's fine."[ix]

Leadership. It is what you want from a quarterback. Dak developed it early in high school and instantly gained respect from his teammates. He motivated them to get better, and he also pushed himself to do the same.

Coaches and teammates described Prescott as extremely competitive and always wanting to be the best in everything he did. He wanted to be on the varsity team as a freshman, but that was not customary. He wanted to be a starter as a sophomore and showed his potential then, but he was not quite ready yet to take the lead, coaches thought. By the time he was a junior, though, the team was Dak's.

Becoming the Leader

He was the heart and soul of Haughton High School—a polite and polished guy that you would love to have as a friend off the field, but a tough, competitive guy who pushed everyone to get better on the field, and definitely someone you hated to play against. He was a guy you would want to go to war with and play hard for. He had the attitude of a winner from day one as a starting quarterback.

During his sophomore season, Prescott played on the junior varsity team. In one of the final games, the varsity coaches came away most impressed with what they saw. Playing rival Airline, Dak made a play where he scrambled to escape pressure and then chucked the ball an astounding 70 yards down the field. The varsity coaches watching could not believe what they had just seen. They knew he was good, but that proved he was even better than they had thought.

"Further than I've ever seen a high school kid throw it," said Prescott's teammate Jason Brotherton.[xlii]

Prescott was moved up to varsity and came in and played from time to time to get some experience. In a playoff game that season, he threw a flea-flicker down the field for a huge completion that led to the game-winning touchdown.

By the end of his sophomore season, people had begun talking about Prescott wherever you went. You could say Haughton was extremely close-knit, sort of like the town of Hickory in *Hoosiers* when it came to basketball. It was not a big town. Football ruled and when the high school team played, people stopped to watch. Ella Chambers, who was neighbors with Prescott when he was in high school, said *everyone* was Dak's family. When he began to win his school games with his exceptional play, Prescott became bigger than the town itself.[xlii]

Prescott's major goal in high school, he said, was to create a legacy for himself. Going in, he was always known as "Tad and Jace's brother." They had incredible athletic ability. Part of separating himself from his brothers was playing a position other than the ones his brothers played. Dak wanted to be a quarterback and thanks to his brother Jace, who taught him how to throw a football growing up, he was quite good at it. At practices, Dak always had a football in his hand wherever he went. It was his brothers, though, along with his mother, who gave him the toughness along with the ambition to be the best in the family. He could—and would—fearlessly take on anything.

One of Haughton's greatest rivals was Parkway, a team that Dak would face twice in the playoffs during his career. In the 2009 District 1-4A Championship, Prescott was enjoying a phenomenal game. He helped lead the Buccaneers to be the first team to score more than 20 points on Parkway all season. However, they still trailed 38-34 with just 1:04 remaining in the game.

"He never looked up," Guin said. "He just said, 'Coach, we got this.'"[xlii]

What transpired over the next minute was a drive that lives on in the Haughton history books. Dak was incredible as he threw completion after completion. In fact, 11 of his 12 passes were caught and the one incompletion was an intentional throwaway, maybe the smartest play of the drive, coaches said. The biggest play of the drive was a third-and-18 where he hit his Fantastic Five friend Jacobs with a hook-and-ladder play, who tossed it to another Fantastic Five player, Jordan Craft. That set up a first down. Then, on the final play, Jim Gatlin, the Parkway coach, realized his team was out of position. Just before he could call timeout, Prescott noticed and snapped the ball. He took advantage of it and connected on a touchdown pass to give Haughton the lead and the win, 41-38.

"Hurry up and graduate," Gatlin said with a laugh, knowing this quarterback was a pain in their side. "You just saw the beginning of someone who was a special leader. He lived for those types of moments."[xlii]

It would not be the last time that Prescott would play Parkway. After his junior season, Prescott began to focus on showcasing his skills for potential colleges. He started the "Dak Prescott World Tour," traveling from state to state in the South and taking part in youth camps to demonstrate his talents for college coaches in the hopes of getting a good scholarship.

But despite how talented Prescott was (and some say he was the best quarterback there), coaches focused on the stars and labeled Prescott as "too slow" or "not polished enough a passer." He could run, but he did not have Justin Fields' speed. He could throw, but he did not have the accuracy of a Trevor Lawrence. After each camp, quarterbacks got put in an exclusive area and invited to their schools for further workouts. Prescott never got an invite.

After camp, they sent out Prescott's highlight tapes to 25 different schools. He got a response from just two, LSU and Mississippi State. Of those two, Mississippi State and new head coach Dan Mullen showed the most interest and that interest would only grow during Dak's senior season. [xlii]

Senior Season

Guin's offense was perfect for Prescott. He ran the spread that was perfectly tailored to Dak's strengths. Dak ran the ball a lot as a quarterback with the option to throw and he excelled. By the end of his high school career, Dak had thrown for more than 5,000 yards and 66 touchdowns. As a senior, he used his legs a lot, running for 950 yards and 17 touchdowns. He was not afraid to go head first, either. He was big and took hits head-on instead of sliding. It made coaches nervous, but that's who Dak was. He was not afraid of anything.[ix]

"He was as good as advertised and played like a man amongst boys," Chris Gillespie said, a former player at LSU who watched Prescott play in high school. "He was bigger than everyone else and was almost impossible to bring down with just one player."[ix]

Gillespie was right. Prescott would drag players on the ground when he ran. He was a monster on the field, not just with his playing ability, but his heart. He left everything on the field and worked harder than anyone. In his first varsity start his junior season, Prescott led what is remembered as a legendary drive down the field, completing a jailbreak fade pass for a touchdown to lead his team to victory.[vii]

In his senior season, Prescott led Haughton to their first-ever undefeated season. Then came the team's District Championship Game against Parkway High School once again. It is a game that people still talk about today as one of the best performances they ever saw in the history of Louisiana High School Football.

Both teams entered the game a perfect 9-0. Mississippi State coaches were there to witness the contest along with a jam-packed stadium at Parkway. What made the game most compelling was the fact that Prescott was injured. He had a torn ligament and meniscus in his knee that he had suffered the game before. The trainer advised him not to play and coaches started him on the sideline, but after a fumble on the opening drive, Guin decided to roll the dice and play Prescott, especially after he was in the coach's ear the entire week begging to play. The opposing school, Parkway, was known for their strong defense and thought that since Prescott could not run he would be easy to shut down.

They were dead wrong.

Prescott threw all over Parkway, and anyone who thought the growing star could not make plays without his legs found out early how good a passer he could be. Prescott ended the game with 366 yards through the air along with four touchdowns to the Fantastic Five.

"People thought that since he couldn't run, Haughton would not be able to win," Gillespie said. "Dak stood in the pocket and just threw all over the secondary...Haughton won by six, but it wasn't even that close of a game."[ix]

Mississippi State offensive line coach John Hevesy was at the game and called Dan Mullen up immediately after the game. "We want this guy on our team." [xlii]

People knew Prescott was going to go to college and be a starter, but it was that game that really made people start to believe that he would not just be a star, but that he also had professional potential. Very few college scouts and head coaches were interested in Dak before that game, but that final game sent the interest in him through the roof. Even LSU wanted him all of a sudden, even though they had told him point-blank the previous summer that he was not good enough to be invited to their school.

There was perhaps no one more in interested than Mullen. Mullen knew he had a mountain to climb to try and persuade Prescott away from LSU, who was now showing interest. Many believed Prescott would end up signing with LSU, but Mullen blew Prescott away in their meeting.

"I saw a young man with an unbelievable work ethic and a desire to be great in everything he does," Mullen said. "I saw that when I was around him. He just has a drive to be great." One of Prescott's heroes was Tim Tebow, who Mullen coached at the University of Florida as the offensive coordinator. Tebow credited Mullen a lot with his development at Florida. Mullen saw a lot of Tebow in Prescott, and given that Mullen's offense was identical not only to what Prescott just ran in high school but also to what Tebow ran at the University of Florida, it was the perfect fit.[ix]

Mullen was an Urban Meyer guy. He coached Alex Smith at the University of Utah when Meyer was head coach there and then followed Meyer to the University of Florida where he worked with Tebow. Because of his success and great coaching prowess, Mississippi State wanted Mullen and he signed with them after Tebow graduated in 2008.

Prescott, who wore number 6 at Haughton simply because that was the jersey that was handed to him, was asked what jersey number he wanted to wear at Mississippi State. It took him less than five seconds to give his answer. "Number 15." That is the jersey number that Tim Tebow wore.

In an interview with the *Dallas News*, Prescott credits the friendship he had with his receivers as a big reason for his success in high school and mentioned how it helped motivate him moving forward.

"I think about moments in high school, I think about the teammates I had in high school and making the relationships the same in the NFL," Prescott said. "I think if I can have half a bit of the relationship off the field in the NFL that we had here in high school, that's a championship team."[ix]

It is an indication of how important Prescott believes chemistry is. How important it is to get along with your teammates and gel together. Teams that win are those that work together and have fun together. It is such a vital part of the game. Patrick Mahomes did not just win a Super Bowl because he was a great quarterback. He won because of the relationship he had with those around him. They respected him and he respected them back. There was a bond there. Prescott believes in that very same thing. You cannot succeed without it. Having those friends around him to throw to in high school and building a relationship with the rest of his team on and off the field helped develop him as both a person and an athlete. It prepared him for the next stages of his life at Mississippi State where he would only continue to turn heads.

Chapter 3: College Career

"Back when I was a senior in high school in Haughton, Louisiana, I had a chance to go to LSU. Everyone I grew up with adored LSU, including my mom. But I chose to come to Mississippi State because I wanted to start a new tradition instead of perpetuating an established one. Since I came here, my teammates and I have had a lot of success on the field, and that has given us a chance to uplift the school and the university."[xi] – Dak Prescott, 2015

Before Dan Mullen and Dak Prescott arrived at Mississippi State University, the football program was in shambles. From 2001 until 2008, the Bulldogs had just one winning season amidst seven seasons where they could not win more than four games. Their record during that span? An ugly 29-65. Mullen began to transform the team as soon as he arrived, taking the team to a 21-17 record from 2009 to 2011, right when Dak Prescott was about to take off the red shirt and make an impact on the Mississippi State roster.[xii]

Prescott first joined the Bulldogs in 2011 but was red-shirted because the team already had a dual-threat senior weapon in Chris Reif and another quarterback as well, sophomore Tyler Russell, who was more of a passing than a running threat. Mullen had the perfect plan for Prescott—to use him exactly how he had used Tim Tebow at Florida.

In 2006, when Tebow was a backup quarterback, he would come in sporadically during the season as a running threat and occasional passing threat. He ran goal-line and short-yardage situations that entire season while Chris Leak, mostly a passing quarterback, started the season and was more of a passing threat.

Prescott was built very similarly to Tebow and Mullen would do the same thing with him in 2012. Russell was the starting quarterback, but Prescott would come in during short-yardage situations and run the ball with an occasional throw here and there. That 2012 season, Prescott was fifth on the team in rushing yards and ran for 4 touchdowns while also throwing for 4 touchdowns on 29 total passes. Russell had a great year, throwing for just under 3,000 yards and 24 touchdowns as the Bulldogs completed an 8-5 record and received an invitation to the Gator Bowl.

Prescott continued to develop under Mullen and established a great relationship with him. The two hit it off immediately, from their first meeting at Dak's house to his prime playing days with Mississippi State. Mullen's quarterback coaching was exquisite, as he had already developed Alex Smith and Tim Tebow into dual-threat college quarterbacks who had set records at their schools.

"Coach Dan Mullen deserves so much credit for what he has done here," Prescott said. "I wouldn't dare for one second to want to play for another college coach. I'm so thankful for him giving me the opportunity to come play at Mississippi State. He and coach John Hevesy saw the talent in me before anyone else; they extended my first major Division I offer. They saw the passion that I play with, the heart all the way back to when I came to camp here. That's what led to them giving me that offer. That's something that I never wanted to get away from. That's who I am. Just for him to give me that opportunity was another reason that I just play with the passion and the effort I do."[xi]

Prescott was humble and always respectful of the men he played for, but especially Mullen. Mullen understood Prescott and made him better each day, both in his playing ability and his leadership on and off the field with the players. Prescott has always said he would never have made it with the Dallas Cowboys if not for Mullen.

That 2013 season would be more of a transition season with Prescott and Russell splitting almost the entire year 50/50. Prescott was not just used as a running threat that season but was also used as a passing threat. Mullen also wanted to use Russell's arm, as he had thrown 24 touchdowns the season before. Eventually, though, Prescott won over the fans in Starkville and became the starting quarterback by season's end, getting the majority of the playing time, especially when Russell was battling injuries. By the time October and November rolled around, Prescott was chucking it 30 to 40 times a game and improving the offense each week.

That season, Prescott led the team in passing with 1,940 yards and a 58.4% completion percentage. While throwing for 10 touchdowns, he led the team in rushing with 859 yards and 13 touchdowns. One of his best performances came in the team's last game of the season. With Russell hurt, the Bulldogs were able to overcome a tough fight from rival team Mississippi in the famed Egg Bowl. Prescott ran for a three-yard touchdown in overtime to help give the Bulldogs the win. Mississippi State football was once again becoming exciting again.[xii]

In the Liberty Bowl against Rice, Prescott was fantastic. He not only threw for three touchdowns but he also ran for two in helping the Bulldogs to a 44-7 rout, setting up what was bound to be a special 2014 season. He was named the Liberty Bowl MVP.[xii]

Dak Prescott was now the captain of the ship, but he faced a rocky schedule ahead. In 2014, it was perceived by many to be a longshot for the Bulldogs to even win eight games. They had three straight matchups against top-10 teams early in the season: LSU, Texas A&M, and Auburn. They also had to face the best team in the country, Alabama, and then an Egg Bowl contest with Ole Miss, who was a national title contender that season and ranked in the top-10. It would not be easy.

Incredibly, Mississippi State did not just win eight games, they won more—all of them—by the end of October. The Bulldogs started that season an incredible 9-0. They won all three games against LSU, Texas A&M, and Auburn. For the first time in school history, Mississippi State was No. 1 in the country in the College Football Playoff poll when the November 11th rankings were revealed. It was the first season of the college football playoffs and Mississippi State had a real shot at winning a spot in the Final Four.[xii]

Those first nine games were some of Prescott's best in his life. Against LSU in Death Valley and in a very hostile atmosphere, Prescott threw for 268 yards while running for 105 in helping the Bulldogs stun the Tigers on their home turf, 34-29. More impressively, he did it in front of family and friends and a school he had turned down. Prescott ran for over 100 yards in four of his first six games in the 2014 season and threw for 14 touchdowns and ran for 8 more in helping his team get off to a 6-0 start. In the team's game against the second-ranked Auburn Tigers at home, Prescott dazzled the home fans by throwing for 246 yards and rushing for 121 as he led his team to a 38-23 upset.[xii]

"One of the things I'm most proud of is we were able to transform the expectations around Mississippi State," Prescott said. "And while people have given me credit for helping change the football culture, what they don't understand is how appreciative I am of my teammates, coaches, the university and the city of Starkville for the role they've played in changing me."[xi]

Very rarely do you hear an athlete use the word "we" as much as Prescott. While many athletes care more about their own performance and love to use the word "I" like it is the only letter in the alphabet, Prescott is different. He always credits others and emphasizes how "we" changed the culture at Mississippi State, not "I." It speaks to the person that Prescott is.

Mississippi State's incredible run that 2014 season came to an end when they played Alabama, a team that had been a thorn in their as well as every other team's side over the last decade. The dynasty led by Nick Saban, though, got a valiant effort from the top-ranked Bulldogs in Tuscaloosa. The Bulldogs entered as an underdog on the road but almost left Alabama with a win. Despite trailing 19-6 entering the fourth quarter, Prescott led a mighty charge and was able to use both his arm and legs to cut the deficit to only five late in the game. However, the Bulldogs could not complete the comeback and lost to the Crimson Tide, 25-20. Prescott showed in that game that he was more than just legs, throwing for 290 yards and 2 touchdowns on the vaunted Alabama secondary.[xii]

Mullen admitted that the game took a lot out of the team. They had tried so hard to win that game and were let down, coming up just short, despite exceeding so many expectations. They still had an outside shot at a playoff spot, but it would be hard with Alabama now controlling their destiny in the SEC West.

Two weeks later in the Egg Bowl and a matchup of two top-10 teams, the Bulldogs were flat. Prescott failed to get anything going on the ground, although he threw for an impressive 282 yards. But the Rebels' home-field advantage was tough to overcome and the Bulldogs lost the Egg Bowl, 31-17. They still finished the season an impressive 10-2 and received their first-ever berth in the Orange Bowl, a New Year's Six bowl game.

In the Orange Bowl against Georgia Tech, however, the defense struggled to contain Paul Johnson's potent option attack. Led by Josh Hamilton, the Yellow Jackets were able to run all over the Bulldogs, despite Prescott and the offense's impressive showing. Prescott had the best passing game yet of his college career, throwing for 453 yards and throwing for 3 touchdowns while also rushing for 1. It was not enough, though, as the Bulldogs lost 49-34.[xii]

Prescott's 2014 season was legendary, and many say that if he had attended a higher-profile school like LSU or Alabama, he may have finished higher than eighth in the Heisman Trophy race. He still had a host of accomplishments that season. He finished on the All-SEC First-Team. He was named an All-American and was a finalist for the Johnny Unitas Golden Arm, Manning, and Davey O'Brien Awards. He was the Manning Award Player of the Week three times and most impressively was named to the All-SEC Honor Roll for his academics.[xiii]

While many thought he should have received more votes in the Heisman Trophy race, he still finished the best of any player in the history of Mississippi State football. Prescott was considered a frontrunner by many for most of the season, but the team's two losses down the stretch hurt his stock quite a bit. Still, he finished the season with 4,435 yards of offense and 41 total touchdowns. The man whose number he wore, Tim Tebow, had finished with 4,181 yards of total offense the year he won the Heisman. Those stats include the players' bowl games. Prescott also broke 10 school records that season, including most combined total yards by a Mississippi State player.[xiv]

For the first time, professional scouts began to turn their eye to Prescott. He was still viewed, however, as more of a running threat, not a passing threat, and that kept him down in the lower ranks of draft boards. Entering the 2015 season, he was viewed more as a backup or a third-string quarterback by the likes of NFL draft experts Mel Kiper and Todd McShay, with a chance to improve that draft stock depending on his play. While 2015 was another great season, it did not do a lot to improve his draft rating. While Prescott flirted with the idea of going professional after the 2014 season, he thought he needed more development in college and wanted to get his degree.

Prescott's main goal in 2015 was to prove he was just as strong a passing threat as he was a running threat. In his first six games that season he ran the ball just 49 times while throwing it 182 times. To compare that with 2014, Prescott ran it 106 times the first six games that season while throwing it 156 times. It was clear that Dak wanted to establish himself more in the passing game. While not running it as much may have cost him some Heisman consideration, he was still leading his team to victories. The Bulldogs got off to another great start in 2015, starting 7-2 and ranked for much of that season despite losing a lot of talent from their 2014 squad. Their only losses those first nine games came to No. 14 LSU and No. 14 Texas A&M (both ranked at that position at the time they played them).[xii]

It was clear, though, as the season went on, that Prescott was trying to establish himself as more of a passer. He had just one 100-yard rushing game that entire season as compared to four the season before.

The Bulldogs had a rough outing against eventual national champion Alabama, losing in Starkville 31-6 in front of a raucous home crowd that left disappointed.

Prescott ended the year with more passing yards than he had the season before. While he only rushed for 588 yards, nearly 400 yards less than the season before, he threw for 3,793 yards, more than 300 than the season before. His completion percentage also increased along with his total touchdowns. He also cut down on his interceptions by more than half, reducing them from 11 to just 5 in 2015. [xii]

While many say his 2015 season was not as impressive as 2014, Prescott would disagree, saying he matured more that final season in college and improved his passing game tremendously. To be successful in the pros, you need to prove yourself as a passer. Prescott had already demonstrated that he could use his legs like Cam Newton or Russell Wilson, who were NFL pro bowlers at the time. He wanted to prove he could use his arm like them as well.

Tragedy

Perhaps the worst moment of Dak Prescott's life came on November 3, 2013. Peggy Prescott, Dak's mother and "bestest" friend, passed away from colon cancer at just 52 years old. Prescott learned of his mother's cancer later than his brothers because they were all so afraid to tell Dak. When Prescott learned of it, it was a tremendous blow. He shaved his hair prior to the 2013 season to support her fight with cancer.

Peggy was a massive inspiration to Dak his entire life and much of what Dak accomplished in his college career could be attributed to her, both in what she did for him as a dedicated parent and in how he played hard for her, wanting to dedicate every game towards her memory.

"When you lose your mom, it's not that easy," Prescott said in 2018. "That's something you've got to wake up every day, looking yourself in the face and knowing that you've got an angel. You've got an angel that has expectations for you to do and you've got to go out there and do them each and every day."[xv]

Prescott achieved the best rushing game of his career the week after his mother's death against Texas A&M and then continued playing his heart out in the Egg Bowl and Liberty Bowl, propelling his team to wins thanks to his extraordinary play. Before his final game at Mississippi State in 2015, Prescott shared his thoughts with the community that helped him through his difficult time.

"That outpouring of support really showed me that to the fans at Mississippi State, I'm not just a good player," Prescott said. "I feel like part of their family because football means so much to them and they reached out to me in that way. It really comforted me. To thank everyone for the support, I came up with a saying: 'We don't have fans, we have family.' I think that sums up how I felt about everyone surrounding Mississippi State during the most traumatic time in my life."[xi]

Any doubts that Prescott ever had about going to Mississippi State over LSU were squashed early on in his college career. They helped lift him up when he needed it and his coaches supported him through his toughest time. Mullen, his teammates, and fellow coaches all comforted him and were by his side during that dark moment and helped him move forward.

"A few weeks after my mom passed in November of 2013, I came back from an injury and entered the Egg Bowl in the second half against Ole Miss," Prescott said. "I'll never forget the feeling when I walked back out on the field. As I walked into the Egg Bowl, the crowd stood up and clapped like they were enveloping me in a giant hug. I've never felt that way before, and I'm not sure I ever will again."[xi]

Prescott went on to call his mother his number one best friend on and off the field as well as the "best coach" he ever had. He still talks to her, saying he talks to her now more than he ever wrote to her, which was pretty much every day in college. "She's always with me. I try to make sure that when people see me, they see my mom's work."[xvi]

Prescott endured more tragedy when his grandfather also passed away during his tenure at Mississippi State. His grandfather played a major role in his life and he used to love visiting him and his grandmother all the time when he was younger. His grandfather had given him a lot of strong words of encouragement and advice when he was faced with racial attacks as a child. Prescott also had to endure an assault while on spring break in March 2015 in Panama City when he and his friends were attending a concert. Prescott was battered and bloodied up but not seriously injured. He took it like a man, though, and instead of using Twitter to bash those who jumped him and his friends, he simply said, "Ignorance happens" and thanked all his fans for the support he received.[xvii]

College was no doubt an up-and-down time for Prescott and a critical period in his life. He had achieved so much during his time as a quarterback and helped transform the culture of his team and in Starkville, but he also had to battle personal tragedy. With the help and love of others, he was able to overcome his tragedies and stay positive, helping pave the way for the next chapter in his life.

The NFL Draft

When Dak Prescott arrived at Mississippi State, he was not sure what his post-college life would be like. When he left there, he knew there was a lot more football to be played, now at the professional level. However, there were a lot of doubters who saw Prescott as nothing more than a career backup or third-string quarterback, if even that. *USA Today's* Scouting report on Prescott was not good: "Dak Prescott has been heralded as one of the more exciting college football quarterbacks to watch during his years at Mississippi State, but a closer examination of the tape shows a prospect with a long way to go if he wants to last in the NFL."[xviii]

In respect to his perceived weaknesses, the first bullet point that was listed simply stated "Inconsistency mars almost every aspect of his game, especially mechanically."[xviii]

That scouting report, along with others, blasted Prescott's accuracy and decision-making and alleged that his "power arm" was not what it was rumored to be. *USA Today* also said in their critique that Prescott was not a good athlete, was heavy-footed, and has no explosiveness whatsoever.[xviii]

The 2016 draft was expected to be a quarterback-heavy draft with Jared Goff and Carson Wentz expected to go with the first two picks. In his three-round mock draft, Kiper had Paxton Lynch, Connor

Cook, Christian Hackenberg all going in the first three rounds with no mention at all of Dak Prescott. Most mock drafts had Prescott going somewhere in the fifth or sixth round, which is where most backup and third-string quarterbacks end up going.

However, some teams were high on Prescott, one of those being the Dallas Cowboys. The Cowboys were looking for a strong backup for Tony Romo, who was 35 years old and entering the later stages of his career. Romo had also battled injury problems in recent years and there was concern about his ability to stay healthy. Many thought the Cowboys would look at taking a quarterback in the first three rounds, one that would eventually supplant Romo in the future. Kiper suggested Paxton Lynch would be a good fit in Dallas.

Not only did the five quarterbacks mentioned above all go by the time the Cowboys picked in the fourth round, so did Jacoby Brissett and Cody Kessler. The Cowboys did initiate a trade attempt to move up in the draft to potentially select Paxton Lynch but the trade failed and the Broncos landed him in the first round with the 26th overall pick. Eventually, it would be the best-failed trade the Cowboys could ever dream of as Lynch never materialized as an NFL quarterback. The Cowboys had been impressed with Prescott after working him out at their practice facility and thought he was a better talent than a lot of the other quarterbacks taken above him. It was great value to get him where they did.[xx]

"This means everything. It was just something I dreamed about," Prescott said. "I ran around the house acting like I was a Cowboys quarterback my whole life, so for it all to come true, it's such a blessing. Just being here with my family, and [owner Jerry] Jones gave me that call, and just the excitement to have my family a majority of Cowboys fans, it was awesome."[xx]

Prescott could not ask for a better place to land. It was not only close to where he grew up, but it was the team he had always loved as a kid. He would now get to back up the quarterback he grew up rooting for if he was able to win the job. He would have to beat out Kellen Moore and Jameill Showers for that job, and eventually Mark Sanchez, who would join the team at the end of the preseason. He would also get to play with the team's No. 1 pick, Ezekiel Elliott, who was considered a star in the making and would prove his worth his rookie season.

Some were not on board with the move, including Kiper, who thought the Cowboys should have tried harder to move up to get Lynch and should have drafted Brandon Allen with the fourth-round pick, not Prescott. Kiper called Prescott "a great guy to have on the bench." Little did Kiper know, Prescott would not be seeing the bench a whole lot.[xix]

Other experts agreed with Kiper, saying Prescott was not worth a fourth-round pick. Joe Klatt of Fox Sports said, "If you're asking me if you have a choice between Dak Prescott and Kevin Hogan, let's say in the later rounds, I think it's a no-brainer—I mean, *no brainer*—that you take Kevin Hogan over Dak Prescott. Prescott is a project, whereas Hogan comes in, sits in the back of the quarterback room, and can be your backup from Day 1."[xix]

Louis Riddick also criticized the move, saying Prescott's accuracy was all over the place and developing him would be a huge job that may not be able to be accomplished.

In May 2016, Prescott went to work to silence his doubters. It would not take long.

Chapter 4: NFL Career

Rookie Season (2016)

When Dak Prescott was asked what jersey number he wanted to wear with the Cowboys, he did not hesitate. He chose number 4 for his mother. His mother's birthday was September 4th. Every time he would step onto the field, Dak would dedicate the game to her and he worked harder than anyone because of what she instilled in him.

During voluntary workouts and offseason training camps, coaches were impressed with what they were seeing early on from Dak Prescott. Jason Garrett, the Cowboys head coach, and starting quarterback Tony Romo said he was easy to mentor and coach since he listened so well and followed through on what he was taught. He learned from his mistakes early and was developing at an extremely fast rate. It continued into training camp as Prescott appeared to be turning heads and had a real chance to win the backup quarterback job.

Of course, for the team itself, there was nowhere to go but up. The Cowboys had finished 4-12 the prior season and underwent a lot of changes in the offseason. The changes were about to become even bigger. During a preseason game against the Seattle Seahawks, Romo broke a bone in his back, an injury that initially was diagnosed to take up to a month to heal. But as time progressed, it was seen as much more severe than initially thought and would end up costing him most of the season. Romo's history of back problems was what caused the bigger concern and he began to contemplate the next move in his career, a decision that was made easier by Prescott's play.[xxi]

The season already looked bleak. At the time Romo got hurt, Prescott had accelerated to the backup quarterback and was now placed No. 1 on the depth chart. In an effort to add some insurance should

Prescott struggle, the Cowboys signed Mark Sanchez, who was let go by the Philadelphia Eagles and whose career was seen as a major disappointment after failing to succeed with the New York Jets earlier in his career.

Fans were in a panic and the media was already calling the season lost. This was a rookie fourth-round pick about to be thrown into the lion's den immediately. There was not much hope or optimism. While Prescott had shown a lot of talent in the preseason and training camp, doing it in real games against starting defenses was a different story. There was a lot of doubt in Big D.

However, there were also reasons to be optimistic. The NFL was changing. Cam Newton was a very similar quarterback in his build and had found success as both a runner and a passer. Russell Wilson also came into the NFL with similar expectations as Prescott and was able to become one of the best quarterbacks in football, helping lead his team to a Super Bowl using both his arm and legs. Given the strict enforcement of defensive secondary penalties, quarterbacks were able to be more aggressive throwing the ball and quarterbacks were excelling earlier in their careers.

Prescott was the fourth-ever Cowboys rookie quarterback to start in his first game. But Cowboys fans had seen this song and dance before. Since Romo had arrived in 2016, they suffered through his injuries and watched veterans like Jon Kitna, Brad Johnson, Kyle Orton, and Brandon Weeden come in and start and the team's record suffered as a result.

Prescott's starting job was only supposed to be temporary. The Cowboys made it clear this was still "Tony's team."[xxi]

On Opening Day, September 11, 2016, Prescott's first start as a Cowboy was seen as a mix of ups and downs. While he exceeded expectations from the fans and the media, the team was unable to start off the season with a win and got out of the gate slow. Prescott was 25-

for-45 for 227 yards, making some great throws while also making some rookie mistakes. He was outshined by Eli Manning, who had thrown for three touchdowns in helping the Giants beat the Cowboys 20-19.[i]

If you would have told Cowboys fans that that would be their last loss until December, they would have laughed so hard in your face your eardrums would be ringing. But something happened after that loss; the Cowboys found something that would carry them to a winning streak that would go into the franchise's record books—and Dak Prescott was at the center of it.

The team's turnaround started with a 27-23 win in Washington, one in which Prescott was nearly flawless as a passer, throwing just 8 incompletions on 30 throws and powering his way to a 6-yard touchdown run in helping lead the Cowboys to a win. Then, against the Bears, Prescott tossed the first touchdown pass of his pro career while also rushing for a touchdown in a two-score win against the Bears.

From there, the touchdown numbers continued to pile up for Prescott. He threw two touchdowns in San Francisco and three in Green Bay. Then two more against the Eagles, three against the Browns, and three against the Ravens, all leading to wins. He was also doing it with his legs, rushing for touchdowns in 5 of his first 11 games. Through 10 games of the season, the Cowboys were 9-1 and Prescott had thrown for 17 touchdowns. He had achieved over a 110-passer rating in 8 of his first 10 starts and was among the leaders in the NFL. Ezekiel Elliott, the team's rookie running back, was also contributing to the team's incredible season, topping 1,000 yards by Thanksgiving.[i]

The Cowboys continued to insist "this is Tony's team," but as the season progressed and Prescott continued to impress, you heard less and less of it from owner Jerry Jones. Fans were beginning to forget about Romo and the media began to put pressure on the Cowboys to reveal what they would do. Could they actually bench a pro bowl quarterback like Romo for a fourth-round rookie?

The questions would only escalate after the team's Thanksgiving game against their rivals, the Washington Redskins. For the fifth time that season, the Cowboys were able to eclipse 30 points behind the arm of Prescott. Prescott tore apart the Redskins by making crucial third-down throws, splitting defenders, and using his legs to extend drives. The Cowboys held off Washington for a 30-26 win, taking the team to 10-1, positioning them well ahead in the NFC East as well as the NFC. Through 11 games, Prescott was 231-for-340 for 2,835 yards and 18 touchdowns while throwing just two picks.[xxii]

Prescott was the talk of the NFL by now. How could draft experts have been so wrong? Mel Kiper had called it a "reach" for the Cowboys to take him in the fourth round. Yet here he was, now doing better than both Jared Goff and Carson Wentz, the two rookies who went with the first two picks. Some doubters were still out there, pointing to the Cowboys' offensive line and Ezekiel Elliott as the real reason behind Prescott's and the Cowboys' success. Sure, the offensive line was doing its job, and having a back like Elliott was good to have, but the sensational numbers that Prescott was putting up could not be ignored and the game on Thanksgiving where he willed his team to victory with his arm and legs had rendered most doubters mum.

Through 11 games that season, Prescott was breaking rookie records. He had the best completion percentage (67.9), interception rate (0.6), quarterback rating (108.6), and adjusted yards per attempt (9.1) for any first-year quarterback through their first 11 games in history.[xxii]

Meanwhile, the Cowboys had a decision looming and one they had to make. With Romo set to come off the injury list, who would be the starter moving forward? But Tony Romo, an athlete filled with class, saw the writing on the wall. He knew if he came back, his back likely would not hold up for that long and he did not want to be a distraction from what Dak Prescott was accomplishing. Romo told the Cowboys that he would accept being a backup to Prescott the rest of the season, not wanting to ruin the chemistry and the run that Prescott was experiencing. He simply wanted to do what was best for the team, and at the time, the best thing was not to mess with what was working.

"Well, I think anybody who's winning that many games, their team was playing so well, I mean that's kind of what will always happen," Romo said. "You just don't mess with that kind of success."[xxiii]

Romo gave a heartfelt speech in front of the media explaining that he would sit on the sidelines and support Prescott. Romo would eventually contemplate retirement, given understandable concerns about not only his back but also his advancing age. On April 4, 2017, Romo retired from the pitch but not the NFL itself, as he moved on to a successful career as an announcer and analyst with CBS, a job he currently holds with Jim Nantz as the top crew for the network.

"Football is really not about any individual, but we all want to be the best," Romo said. "One of the major reasons you're winning and being great. You know, as you become a dad and you get older, you can kind of see there are rare multiple sides. It's just not about me. It's about so many more people. I just feel like when your team is playing well and everybody is playing really good football, it's just a team sport. It's not about an individual."[xxiii]

Say what you will about Tony Romo, but he is one of the classiest athletes to ever play the game, and what made the Cowboys so great was that Dak Prescott was also just as classy. The two of them respected each other and helped one another when they needed to. Prescott has always been grateful to Romo for acting as a mentor to him that first season and said that he would not have been the quarterback he was in that first year or now if it were not for Romo. Both players put the team first, and when you have those kinds of athletes on your team, it is a great thing.

With Prescott now in full command, the Cowboys continued their winning ways. They extended their winning streak to 11 games by going to Minnesota and winning on their home field, 17-15. The Vikings defense, the best in football, was able to contain Prescott—but not enough— as he threw for a touchdown, leading his team to an 11-1 record.[i]

Prescott was on cloud nine by this point in his career and enjoying incredible success. The media could not stop praising him. He had given Cowboys fans "Prescott Fever." But he was brought back down to earth a bit by the Giants the following week in what would be one of his worst games as a pro and the worst game of his rookie season. Prescott could not get anything going in New York. He threw two interceptions in that game, which was as many as he had thrown in all of his first 12 games. He had a 45.9 passer rating and completed just 17 passes in 37 attempts. It was an awful performance and the Cowboys streak finally ended with a 10-7 loss to the Giants.

Sometimes games like that can be a good thing, though. Reality sets in a bit and reminds you of where you are in the world. Getting "too confident" can have its effects and Prescott was reminded that it is not an easy game.

How you bounce back from those bad moments help define who you are. The weak let it get to them while the strong learn from it and come back hungrier and fiercer than before. Prescott did just that in his next game against the Tampa Bay Buccaneers, a game that firmly established him as the future of the Dallas Cowboys. From one of his worst just the week before,

Dak turned it around and had one of the best games a rookie quarterback could ever aspire to.

Prescott was flawless. He threw 36 passes, throwing just 4 incompletions, and finished with an 88.9 completion percentage. He dazzled the home crowd by escaping trouble and making plays, throwing for 279 yards and rushing for a touchdown in a 26-20 victory over the Bucs. It was a statement victory that put the Cowboys right back on track for the top seed in the NFC.[i]

After a three-touchdown performance against the Lions, Prescott and the Cowboys wrapped up home-field advantage and tied the record for most wins in a season in Cowboys history (13). They sat most of their starters in the final game when they could have broken the record with Prescott only playing a handful of series. The team's backups mostly played and they lost to the Eagles, finishing the year 13-3 and getting a first-round bye in the playoffs.

It was an amazing, Cinderella season for Prescott. He threw for 3,367 yards, throwing 23 touchdowns and finishing with a 67% completion percentage. He also ran for 282 yards and combined for 29 touchdowns rushing and passing. He joined a short list of rookie quarterbacks to make the Pro Bowl. Prescott finished the season 4th in completion percentage, 3rd in lowest interception percentage, 3rd in quarterback rating, and 4th in net yards gained per pass attempt.[i]

A lot of people were perplexed. How did so many people miss the boat on this guy? Despite being projected to be among the lowest quarterbacks drafted in the 2016 class, Prescott finished as the *best*. He outshined every rookie quarterback in the league— along with most other veteran quarterbacks of the game as well.

The answer lies in who Prescott is. The coaches on the Cowboys were certainly not surprised after what they saw of Prescott prior to preseason. This was a guy who worked harder than anyone. He woke up at 6 a.m., went to the practice facility, and trained. When he was not training with his team, he was training with family, friends, or teammates. Even his aunt, Paige Gilbeaux who works for SportsStar Recreation in Houston, helped him.[xxiv] "I lost 10 pounds helping him," she joked. "He worked me to death."[xxiv]

Prescott proved that if you want something badly enough and you work hard at it, you can earn it. Prescott wanted to not just prove doubters wrong, he wanted to be a starting quarterback one day for the Dallas Cowboys. While he did not think it would come this fast, he was ready for the opportunity because of how hard he worked.

Offensive coordinator Scott Linehan said he and head coach Garrett put Prescott through hell to catch him up to speed. While most players would dread the workouts, Linehan said Prescott enjoyed it. He loved working hard and knowing that he was getting better.

Quarterback coach Wade Wilson said he learned the playbook faster than any quarterback he had ever coached in his 10 years and said he had a confidence and aura about him that was unmatched.[xxiv]

Prescott's hard work paid dividends. He not only got the keys to become the Dallas Cowboys' starting quarterback from 2016 on, but he was also named the 2016 AP Offensive Rookie of the Year, beating out teammate Ezekiel Elliott. Unfortunately, the season ended on a sour note for the team when they ran into Aaron Rodgers and the Packers' elite offense. Prescott was solid, going 24-for-302 yards and 3 touchdowns, perhaps his best game of the season. But the Cowboys defense could not contain Aaron Rodgers, who made mind-boggling throws, especially on the final drive of the game which set up a game-winning field goal. The Packers eliminated the Cowboys in the Divisional Round, 34-31.[i]

While it was not the way Prescott wanted his season to end, he defied so many expectations and made experts like Mel Kiper and the draft scouts at *USA Today* eat crow. It was one of the best rookie seasons ever, perhaps even the most impressive rookie year in history for a player drafted so late. Most exceptional rookie seasons come from first-round guys, not fourth-rounders. What Prescott did was special. And it was only the beginning.

Sophomore Slump (2017)

There is no such thing as avoiding adversity. Rollercoasters go up and down, and it is how you fight through the downtimes and overcome moments of difficulty that define you. The 2017 season was not an easy one for Dak Prescott. Expectations were very high going in and the pressure was overwhelming. When you play on a team like Dallas, "America's Team," people expect greatness out of you all the time. While fans did not expect another 13-3 season, they did anticipate another division title and a Super Bowl run. They got anything *but* that.

Sophomore slumps are all too common. Sometimes after a breakout rookie season, you feel on top of the world—then the world brings you right back down. You think things are going to work just as easily and they just do not. But it is important to learn lessons from it and Prescott did just that.

"It (2017) made me respect this league, the game, the preparation, and everything it takes to be great in this league so much more," Prescott said. "Having a first year like I did, I think you almost want to take things for granted. And then you come in the second year and a lot of things just go against you and it's tough. On the field, off the field—you have to battle through it, and I feel like I've done that. I've given my all; I'll learn from it and get better."[xxv]

Overall, the 2017 season was not all bad. Prescott had some great moments. The biggest difference was that he took a few more chances with his throws and, unfortunately, it cost him. After throwing just four interceptions the season before, he threw 13 in 2017. He went from the third-lowest in interceptions in 2016 to seventh-highest in 2017. He also dropped from fourth to 13th in completion percentage. His quarterback rating of 86.6 was good for 17th. It just was not as easy.[i]

So, what caused the change? A lot of it had to do with teams having more tape on him and being able to devise game plans to contain him. They say it is hard to plan for rookie quarterbacks, but it easier in the second year once they have had time to view film on the guy and scheme against him. Then, the third year, that quarterback many times will figure it out and rise above, which would be the case for Dak. The team around him, though, also was not as strong. The team faced some injuries, including to star running back Ezekiel Elliott and star offensive tackle Tyron Smith. And defensively, they struggled to stop teams. The

Cowboys gave up 42 points, 35 points, and 35 points respectively in three of its first five games, which got them off to a 2-3 start out of the gate.

The Cowboys and Prescott finished strong, though. After starting 5-6, the team rallied to win 4 of its last 5 to finish 9-7, just shy of making the postseason. Overall that season, Prescott still threw for 3,324 yards, a solid season for a second-year quarterback, although shy of his 2016 numbers. He became the first Cowboys quarterback in history to throw for over 3,000 yards in each of his first two seasons as a starter. But there were other numbers that were not so good. He had seven games where he failed to throw for 200 yards, compared to just three from his rookie season. He also averaged just 6.8 yards per pass attempt compared to 8 yards per attempt a season ago.[xxv]

There was also the offensive line that did not protect him as well as it did a year ago. With Smith hurt, Prescott faced a lot more pressure and did not have as much time to throw the ball. It showed. Against the Atlanta Falcons that season, Prescott was sacked eight times. The Seahawks sacked him four times and rushed and hurried him much more. Not having that critical time in the pocket hurts any quarterback, no matter how good you are.[xxv]

"It was just a lot of mental mistakes, a lot of things that I felt like I don't normally do," Prescott said. "I thought a lot about different things within the games. It's something that I'm going to try to eliminate going forward."[xxvi]

Prescott acknowledged his rough season, knew what he did wrong, and set out to fix it. Coaches, teammates, family, and friends knew he would bounce back based on who he was. Prescott was a workaholic. He did not accept failure well. He would work as hard as he possibly could before the 2018 season to get his stature back as one of the best up-and-coming quarterbacks in the NFL and bring the Cowboys back to the postseason.

Redemption (2018)

"I had high expectations for myself last year and didn't meet them, so it's about raising those expectations and doing everything I can to make sure that I surpass my expectations."[xxvi] – *Dak Prescott, 2017*

Prescott was competitive. He wanted to be the best. He knew expectations were not just high on him from others, they were high on him from *himself*. He always challenged himself to get better and go above and beyond. He did that in high school, in college, and his rookie professional season. His second year did not go as well and he accepted his mistakes and understood that it is part of the learning process. 2018 would be his chance to prove to himself and the world that he had learned from his mistakes and overcome them.

The media was not easy on him. After all, the Dallas Cowboys are the New York Yankees of the NFL. If you do not live up to the hype, the media and the fans get on you. People were questioning whether Prescott was really that good, or whether he was just a product of a good supporting cast around him. They always go hand-in-hand, though. Having a good supporting cast is important for every quarterback, and vice-versa. You cannot point to a Hall-of-Fame quarterback who succeeded with a bad supporting cast. Joe Montana always had Jerry Rice. Peyton Manning had the best offensive line in football. Terry Bradshaw had Lynn Swann and John Stallworth.

Having Tyron Smith back in 2018 was huge. While Prescott never cited injuries as an excuse, those who dig deep into the struggles of 2017 will see that not having Smith there hurt him. Prescott made mental mistakes, but a lot of those were caused by not having the protection and time to throw. It was good to have him back that third season.

The season would not start easy, though, and the supporting cast got thinner. Two of his go-to guys abruptly were gone. First, Jason Witten announced his retirement. Then, the team released Dez Bryant, the team's leading wide receiver. But Prescott took it in stride and just went about his business. The media asked him who would step up in place of the two Pro Bowlers now gone from the lineup.

"I think it'll just happen (someone stepping up)," Prescott said. "I think in certain games against certain defenses, it'll be a certain guy. It'll be a different guy...So when you have a corps like that, hopefully it's a different guy every game just to keep the defense on their toes."[xxvi]

While Prescott never publicly said it, not having Bryant might have been a good thing. In three games Bryant missed in 2016, Prescott threw for six touchdowns and rushed for one. With him in the lineup for almost all of 2017, he was not as good. Bryant was one to get in your ear a lot if you did not throw him the ball, only adding to the pressure on Prescott. He could be more relaxed without that problem in 2018.

The 2018 season started slowly, though. The Cowboys were obviously lacking playmakers early on. They got off to an ugly 3-5 start, which included scoring just 8 points against the Panthers, 13 against the Seahawks, 17 against the Redskins, and 17 against the Titans. Prescott threw for under 200 yards in 4 of his 6 games and had 10 touchdowns alongside 5 picks. Not having Bryant and Witten there were taking its toll. The supporting cast just was not there for him to throw to. At wide receiver, the Cowboys had Allen Hurns, Michael Gallup, and Cole Beasley, three guys who were good supporting wide receivers, but just not enough. And at tight end, Geoff Swaim was clearly not Jason Witten.

Jerry Jones and the organization realized this and made a bold move to give Prescott some help. On October 22nd, with the Cowboys sitting at 3-4, the team traded a first-round pick in 2019 to acquire Raiders wide receiver, Amari Cooper. While some chided the move, saying that Cooper was not as good as he was hyped to be, others said he was not in a good situation in Oakland and he would be better in a different setting. As it turned out, he was better in Dallas. He was just what the struggling Cowboys needed.

Prescott immediately clicked with Cooper as the team found its number one receiver. His addition also made Beasley and Gallup better because defenses swarmed more to Cooper. After a 3-5 start, the Cowboys went 7-1 in the second half of the season. Having Cooper was like a switch for Prescott. His numbers flipped. He had just one game under 200 yards the rest of the season, a game in which they dominated mostly on the ground against the Bucs.[i]

One of Prescott's best games came against the Super Bowl champion Eagles who were challenging the Cowboys for first place in the division. Prescott was phenomenal and really proved himself as one of the best quarterbacks in the league during that game. Prescott went 42-for-54 for 455 yards, his best game ever as a professional. He threw for three touchdowns while running for another. Tied at 23 in overtime, Prescott led the team down the field from the opening tick in the extra period. Needing a touchdown to win, Prescott hit Amari Cooper on a perfect 15-yard pass that lifted the Cowboys to a 29-23 victory over the Eagles. The win put the Cowboys 8-5 and in first place in the NFC East. It was also their second win against their rivals that season and their fifth win in a row.[i]

In those final 8 games, Prescott threw 12 touchdown passes and just 3 interceptions. His passer rating shot up and he had multiple games where he had a rating over 120, something he failed to do the first half of the season. His completion percentage, which was hovering in the low 60s the first half of the season, shot up into the 70s the second half of the year. [i]

The Cowboys finished the season on a high note, beating the Giants 36-35 at MetLife Stadium to give them some momentum going into the postseason.

Prescott continued to elevate his game, throwing for 387 yards and 4 touchdowns. Prescott threw 11 touchdowns in his final 6 games, and all of a sudden, the Cowboys had Super Bowl aspirations behind Prescott.

Those aspirations grew stronger after an incredible wildcard round game against Seattle at home. Trailing 6-3 late in the first half, Prescott led Dallas on a seven-play, 75-yard drive that culminated in an 11-yard strike to Michael Gallup just before halftime, giving the Cowboys a 10-6 halftime lead. Then with the game 17-14 in the fourth quarter, Prescott again led the Cowboys down the field, trying to give them an insurance score. Using his arm and legs, Prescott led them 63 yards down the field with the clock running down and finished the drive off with a one-yard touchdown run. Dallas went ahead 24-14, and despite a late Seahawks score, the Cowboys hung on for a 24-22 win.

Players and coaches did not hold back on how much Prescott helped lead the team in that game. True leadership was illustrated by the Cowboys' young quarterback.

"He showed that he won this playoff game," owner Jerry Jones said. "He took it on his shoulders. He made plays that put us in position to come out like we did. That is what you want from your quarterback."[xxvii]

"It's simple. He's a grown a** man," running back Ezekiel Elliott added. "He led us to the win tonight. He carried us on his shoulders."[xxvii]

To get that kind of respect from the leader of your organization and your teammates speaks volumes about the job that Prescott did and how well he was developing as a leader. Head coach Jason Garrett also praised Prescott after the game, crediting his poise under pressure and his ability to make plays and lead the team.

The Cowboys' impressive season, unfortunately, came to an end in Los Angeles the following week. Despite helping the Cowboys to an early lead and playing a solid game at quarterback, Prescott and the Cowboys could not find a way to get the ball away from the Rams' formidable offense. The Rams dominated on the ground, getting over 100-yard rushing performances from both Todd Gurley and C.J. Anderson. Prescott tried to lead the team back late but fell just short. The Rams moved on to the NFC Championship with a 30-22 win.

It was still a great year for Dak Prescott, who shook off a rough start to the season. He threw for 3,885 yards—his best season yet—tossed 22 touchdowns, and accumulated a 96.9 passer rating. He made his second pro-bowl appearance in Orlando where he got a quarter of playing time. However, conditions were miserable. The Pro Bowl in Orlando was played in a driving rainstorm with heavy winds and temperatures in the low-to-mid 40s, very unusual for Florida. A usually packed stadium was half-empty. Prescott threw a touchdown and interception in the game, but the weather was so bad, officials used a running clock to try and get out of the miserable weather as soon as possible.

Prescott was nominated for the Walter Payton Man of the Year Award that season, an incredible honor that recognizes not just playing ability, but sportsmanship and respect for the game and the NFL community both on and off the field. More honors would be coming his way in the 2019 season.

Breaking Out (2019-2020)

The Cowboys had high hopes for the 2019 season after very nearly landing themselves in the NFL's Final Four in 2018. Prescott was determined to develop further and worked harder than he ever had in the offseason, working on improving his passing skills. Coaches wanted to use his arm more and utilize the team's strong wide receivers. Amari Cooper and

Michael Gallup were back and Jason Witten returned from retirement eager to work with Prescott. Ezekiel Elliott held out during training camp but reported just before the team's first game after reaching a new deal with the team.

In the team's opening game against the Giants, Prescott was spectacular. He was 25-for-32 for 405 yards and tossed 4 touchdown passes in the Cowboys blowout 35-17 win. He set a career-high passer rating of 158.3. He then followed that up with two more impressive performances, tossing three touchdowns against the Redskins and two against the Dolphins as Dallas got off to a 3-0 start. The talk had already started of a Most Valuable Player Award. He was that good.[i]

After that, though, things cooled down a bit and Prescott went through a cold stretch. Their first loss came at the hands of New Orleans as the Saints held them to just 10 points and managed to steal the win with just 12 points themselves. Defensively, the Cowboys were struggling, too, especially in their next matchup in Green Bay. Despite throwing for a career-high 463 yards against the Packers, Prescott also tossed 3 interceptions. Meanwhile, the defense could not find a way to stop Aaron Rodgers. They also had a poor offensive showing against the Jets. After a 3-0 start, the Cowboys were sitting at 3-3.[i]

The season was up-and-down from there, but Prescott was back to form and putting up numbers like he never had. The offense was a juggernaut, but the defense continued to struggle. Prescott added another 400-yard performance in Detroit in Week 11 and had seven 300-yard games on the season. To put that in perspective, Prescott had just two 300-yard games the season before. Through the first half of the 2019 season, Prescott continued to be among the leaders in the NFL Most Valuable Player race.[i]

The Cowboys finished 9-7, which unfortunately kept them just out of the postseason as they trailed the Eagles by a game in the NFC East. Prescott ended the season with 4,902 yards, shattering his old career-high with the team and finishing No. 2 in the NFL in total yards. His final game of the season included a four-touchdown performance in a 47-16 win over the Redskins. He finished just one yard short of Tony Romo for most passing yards ever in a season by a Dallas Cowboy.[i]

Alongside finishing second in total passing yards in the league, Prescott finished fourth in touchdowns thrown (30), fourth in total completions (388), second in first-down passing (229), and fifth in overall quarterback rating (72.8). His outstanding season surprisingly did not land him in the Pro Bowl, however, mostly because of how good the other quarterbacks in the NFC also were. Trying to beat out Drew Brees, Aaron Rodgers, and Russell Wilson is a tough task.

The Cowboys' tumultuous season led to some changes. The team fired head coach Jason Garrett and hired former Packers coach Mike McCarthy to lead the team. The team also gave Prescott another weapon to throw to by drafting Oklahoma standout CeeDee Lamb, who had shined as a rookie.

After the season, talks began about Prescott's future with the team. Prescott was to be a free agent soon but the Cowboys did not want to lose him. Because of COVID-19, a global health pandemic that had caused a great deal of upheaval in the world of professional sports, it made it more difficult to sign the quarterback to a long-term deal prior to the start of free agency. As a result, the Cowboys placed a franchise-tag on Prescott, allowing him to stay on the team for one more year while they could further negotiate a contract. The holdup seemed to be a four-year versus a five-year commitment. Also, trying to stay under the salary cap with so many other big contracts on the team presented an obstacle in working out a deal.

"We're talking about a situation where he's going to represent so much of your salary cap," Vice President Stephen Jones said. "I think he understands where we're coming from. We're trying to get in a situation where we can keep Dak surrounded by great players."[xxviii]

It can be hard to work deals when you have so many great players on the roster. The salary cap keeps the NFL from having "Super Teams" like the NBA has. You cannot just sign a bunch of superstars. You need to stay under a salary cap limit. With the Cowboys' Ezekiel Elliott, Amari Cooper, Tyron Smith, Zack Martin, Leighton Vander Esch, and DeMarcus Lawrence already occupying so much of the cap, it made the task that much more difficult to work out a deal. However, Stephen and Jerry Jones both had the same goal in mind: to build a future team around the Cowboys' star quarterback. And the feelings were mutual—Dak Prescott undoubtedly wanted to remain a Cowboy, as did his teammates.

A Season-Ending Injury

In 2020, Prescott picked up right where he left off in 2019. In his first four games, he threw for 266 yards, 450 yards, 472 yards, and 502 yards respectively. Unfortunately, like 2019, the team's defense went through struggles and the team got off to a poor start. But Prescott was clearly moving in the right direction and progressing as a passer. In fact, he was leading the league with 1,690 yards when his progress came to an unexpected and horrific end.

On October 11th, in the third quarter of a hard-fought game against the New York Giants, Dak Prescott suffered a gruesome compound fracture and dislocation to his right ankle. As Giants' defensive back Logan Ryan dragged Prescott down in a tackle, their legs became entangled and Prescott's foot became caught under Ryan's leg. The resultant severe injury, not just a broken ankle but bone puncturing skin, was the kind of thing you wince and avert your eyes away from. Prescott was carted off the field in tears and his season was suddenly over.

The Cowboys actually won that fateful game against the Giants, but what they lost was of much greater significance. America's Team would now be at the mercy of backup quarterbacks Andy Dalton, and later, Garrett Gilbert, to finish out the season. 2020 was shaping up to be a year that the Cowboys as well as much of a struggling and lackluster NFC East would be happier to forget.

Dak Prescott underwent surgery immediately following the injury and by all reports is well on the mend. It is unknown at this time how quickly he will be able to return and resume the mantle of leader, but the initial recovery time has been estimated at four to six months.

The Cowboys organization is, nonetheless, very optimistic about his future with the franchise.

"You knew right away it was serious," Cowboys coach Mike McCarthy said. "I feel terrible for him. He was having a tremendous year in just a short time working with him. He's made such an impression on me, and he's clearly the leader of this football team. I have no doubt that he'll bounce back from this and this will be a part of his great story. This will just be another chapter in a great story. He's a fine young man and an outstanding quarterback."[xliii]

When asked about his future with the team, Stephen Jones confidently declared that Prescott "is our future" and owner Jerry Jones was equally supportive, staunchly affirming that they had no reservations about keeping Dak firmly in place as their leader.

Dak himself has been nothing but upbeat and positive in the wake of this setback. "I'll be back stronger and better," he recently posted on Instagram as he thanked his fans for all their love and support.

This was Dak Prescott's first serious injury, as he had never even been on IR prior to that incident. As a strong, tough-as-nails, and otherwise healthy 27-year-old, we expect to see this remarkable young phenom back to form and back on the field in the 2021 season.

Chapter 5: Personal Life

Difficult Times

"Our adversity, our struggles, what we go through, it's always going to be too much for ourselves," Prescott said. "It may be too much for one or two people. But it's never too much for a community or for the people in the family you love. So we have to share those things."[xxxii] –Dak Prescott, 2020

Football is Dak Prescott's passion and also an escape from a tumultuous life filled with a lot of ups but also a lot of downs. His ankle injury was far from the first difficulty in his life that he has had to overcome. Indeed, it has not been an easy path and it is incredible how he has succeeded, given all that has happened around him. As documented, Prescott's early childhood was not like many star athletes. He grew up in poverty and in a trailer park. He fought off racial prejudice in his neighborhood and had to work hard to earn respect.

He had done that in high school and college, but tragedies kept getting in the way. His mother and grandfather both passed while he was at Mississippi State. His mother's death, especially, was tragic and thankfully all the support he received was able to pull him out of a deep hole. But then more tragedy struck. On April 24, 2020, Dak's brother Jace died of an apparent suicide.

Between this and the coronavirus pandemic, which has kept many athletes locked up in quarantine and forced so many of us to get through mental challenges of our own, Prescott suffered a difficult bout with depression in the spring of 2020. His brother was a huge influence on him and helped him a lot after his mother died. Without him by his side, and without others being able to reach out to him because of the pandemic, Prescott was feeling isolated and was hurting more than anyone knew.[xxix]

"Honestly, a couple of days before my brother passed, I started experiencing depression," Prescott said. "I didn't know what I was going through, to say the least, and hadn't been sleeping at all. But for one night, I sleep the best I've slept, missing 10-plus calls from Tad and giving my dad enough time to come in my bedroom and tell me what happened. So, I woke up after the best night of sleep I've had in 2020 from the worst news—some of the worst news I'll ever get."[xxix]

It could be said that any person or athlete would go through just what Prescott went through. Many athletes have suffered depression before but kept it bottled up inside. Prescott thought it best to tell his story in an effort to inspire others to get help when they begin to feel depressed. It was a dark time for Dak when his brother died.

"When you have thoughts that you've never had, I think that's more so than anything a chance to realize it and recognize it, to be vulnerable about it," Prescott said. "Talked to my family, talked to the people around me simply as I did at the time. Some of them obviously had dealt with it before, was able to have those conversations and then reach out further just to more people."[xxix]

Prescott's hope was that speaking out would help others when they experience depression. It is nothing to be afraid of. There are people out there to help you. If Dak did not get help right away, it could have gotten worse. He hopes that others realize this moving forward. He has since visited others who have gone through depression, telling his story and trying to brighten their spirits. He knows what it is like to experience pain and dark times. He wants to be a helping voice because that is who Dak is. Some talk about depression but do not know what it feels like. They just say what they say because that is what they are told to say. But not Dak. He knows the feeling. He knows the struggle.

"Mental health is a huge issue and a real thing in our world right now, especially in the world we live in where everything is viral and everyone is part of the media," Prescott said. "(You) can get on social media and be overcome with emotions and thoughts of other people and allow that to fill in their head when things aren't necessarily true, whether it is getting likes on Instagram or something being viewed or getting bullied or whatever it may be."[xxix]

A few people in the media have unkindly criticized Dak for being so open and honest about his feelings. For the most part, however, Dak has the love and support of fans and colleagues throughout the NFL and around the world. He has been applauded for his outspoken efforts and many supporters have come forward to chastise those critics who suggested that he should hide those feelings. Dak has said that would make him a fake person and that is not who he is. Leaders do not hide anything.

"Being a leader is about being genuine and being real," he said. "Before I even lead, I have to make sure my mind is in the right place to do that and lead people to where they want to be. I think that is important—to be vulnerable, to be genuine and to be transparent."[xxix]

Charity Work and Endorsements

Dak's off-the-field work is one of the most respectable things about him. He has turned tragedy into triumph by helping lead the Faith, Fight, Finish Charity Foundation. His mother and brother motivated him to start the organization, which helps families facing cancer. The charity is meant to honor his mother, Peggy.[xxx]

Prescott also has raised money to combat racism in society. In June 2020, he pledged a million dollars to help fight systematic racism after the death of George Floyd, which has caused a lot of social unrest in the country lately. He also pledged money to help improve the training of police officers so these events never happen again. While Prescott has kept his politics out of it, he wants to help those who have faced prejudice, much like he did as a child.

Prescott also runs youth football camps across the South. He runs one back in his hometown of Haughton, Louisiana, another one at Mississippi State, and a third in Austin, Texas. All the camps help young football players develop and take them through the skills and drills to become better players. It is here where he gets the chance to reunite with "The Fantastic Five," his best friends from when he was younger. They help him with the camp back home and it gives them a chance to have fun and reflect on their younger playing days together.

While Prescott's current salary is not very much (which could change pending a new deal), his endorsement deals have aided his income a great deal. Prescott made just $2 million in 2019 on the field, but off the field, Prescott made nearly $50 million off endorsements, according to Cowboys Newswire.[xxxi]

Some of Prescott's more popular endorsements include Campbell's Chunky Soup, 7-Eleven, New Era, Sleep Number, Oikos, Pepsi, and Citibank. Prescott uses some of the money he earns from endorsements to help sponsor his football camps and provide money towards the charities that he runs.

Dak's Free Time

Prescott has done a good job at keeping his private life private, even though he has been linked to several women over the years. Much like Derek Jeter did in the earlier years of his career with the Yankees, Prescott has taken advantage of not being married and achieving stardom. He has been associated with Ireland Borba, Yasmine Lee, and Kayla Puzas, among others.

As of this writing, Prescott is dating Instagram model Natalie Buffett, but not much is known of their relationship as of yet. They made their status as a couple known on social media in July 2020.[xxxii] In October they poked some fun at Dak's ankle injury—he dressed up for Halloween as a patient and she, his nurse.

Like any young athlete, Prescott does like to have his fun. He hangs out with his friends in the offseason and likes to socialize. He made the news recently in a not-so-flattering way when he received some criticism for throwing a party that did not provide enough social distancing given the dangers of the COVID-19 pandemic.[xxxii]

Prescott is also known to be a big Kanye West fan. One of the famous stories about Prescott is how he once improbably turned down free tickets to a West concert to try and catch up on sleep when he was deprived of it. According to the story, Prescott was a rookie and working hard to try and improve as the team's new starting quarterback. With Kanye performing in Dallas, Prescott knew that he would be out late and be hungover for practice the next day if he attended. So instead, Prescott relaxed and watched Thursday night football and rested up for preparation and the game on Sunday. "I wanted to go, but I just think about the *perception* of it all. And I love my sleep," Prescott said.[xxxiii]

Prescott is also big into fishing, as are many that grew up in Louisiana. Prescott's Instagram is filled with pictures of him fishing in Louisiana from the days when he was younger up until now. He even passed up a chance to appear on late-night television and add some endorsement money just to go fishing and spend time with his grandma. It has become one of his favorite pastimes over the years.[xxxiv]

One of Prescott's biggest passions is his love for dogs. He posts pictures of himself with his pitbull, Legend, all the time on Instagram. He also had a yellow lab that he recently gave to a family friend. The dog's name?

Tibeaux, in honor of his favorite college quarterback, Tim Tebow.

Dak's Father

While Dak has been very vocal about the impact his mother and brother played in his life, both of whom passed away during his playing days, not much is known about his father, Nathaniel Prescott, who goes by "Nat."[xxxviii] But the rumors out there about him shrugging off his son were disputed by Dak himself, and those who know the two on a more personal level are aware that Nathaniel has also played a positive role in Dak's life. It is just a different role compared to what his mother played.

Like Peggy Prescott, Nat struggled to make a living early during Dak's life. He went through a few jobs trying to make ends meet and moved around quite a bit. But he has always stayed in contact with his son and is known as "Pops" to Dak. On Dak's 24th birthday, Nat surprised him with a birthday party.

"It was cool," Dak said. "It was a surprise. I usually don't get surprised, so they pulled that one off. I congratulated them on that one because he has tried too many times and it doesn't work. He got me on that one. It was good for him. I was excited more for him with him being a longtime Cowboys fan. The history of being out here in Oxnard, just coming out here and watching us practice."[xxxviii]

Nat moved to Dallas a few years back to be closer to his son and watch him play football for a team he had always grown up loving. Dak himself was a Cowboys fan growing up because that was who his father loved.

Every relationship is different. Some fathers watch out for their sons every step of the way while others let them develop and discover who they are and do not try to get in the way. Nat was more hands-off with his son, knowing all the time that he had a close relationship with his mom and that she would do a good job bringing him up, but he always stood by him and cheered him on, reaching out to him as much as he could and supporting him every step of the way.

"Me and my dad have always had a tight relationship, different from my brothers, I guess," Dak said. "But we all have our own individual relationships. He has always been there for me."[xxxviii]

Chapter 6: Legacy

One of Dak Prescott's biggest legacies is that he is part of the new generation of NFL quarterbacks that includes Russell Wilson, Cam Newton, Lamar Jackson, Josh Allen, and Kyler Murray. These are a new breed of players that can make plays with their arms and their legs. Through his first five years in the NFL, Dak Prescott has been doing just that, although it has been more his arm that has impressed fans, while scouts thought he would be more of a running quarterback. He has used his legs when needed to, but overall, he has become a pass-first quarterback and a dangerous threat with that arm.

Prescott has already joined an elite group of Cowboys and quarterbacks. He has thrown for more yards than any Cowboys quarterback in history over their first four full seasons, with 15,478 yards. Additionally, he broke Tom Brady's record in 2016 for most pass attempts without an interception to begin a career when he went an amazing 176 throws without a pick. Prescott also became the first player ever to throw for over 400 yards while rushing for 3 touchdowns when he did it on September 19, 2020, in the team's incredible come-from-behind win against the Falcons at home.[xxxv]

Additionally, Prescott broke the record for best interception rate for a quarterback in his first 50 starts, throwing just one pick every 59.1 attempts. "Greatness is consistency," wide receiver and teammate Amari Cooper said. "For him to be that consistent is pretty remarkable."[xxxvi]

Prescott's development is a testament to how hard he worked to get from a fourth-round draft pick, someone who was passed over several times, to now be a starting quarterback and one of the most respected players in the league. So, what helped Prescott develop so rapidly? Prescott credits his workout regimen and an improvement in his flexibility for his breakout play in 2019. He did an incredible amount of workouts and drills in the offseason to keep improving.[xxxvi]

It is too early to tell what kind of player Prescott will be remembered as when he retires, but one thing is for sure: there aren't many quarterbacks in history who will have put in the time and work that Prescott does. His old head coach, Jason Garrett, says the guy does nothing but work hard and improve.

"It goes back to who he is, right from the start—our experience with him as a rookie," Garrett said. "He's a very purposeful guy. He comes to work every day and he wants to get better in all phases. People always ask about his improvement, and where he's improved the most—it is across the board. He works on the technique, footwork, and release, and how that factors into how well he throws the ball, how accurately he throws the ball. There isn't a day that goes by that he doesn't try to get better."[xxxvi]

Prescott's next goal is to try to build a consistent winner and Super Bowl champion. Playing on the Cowboys comes with a lot of pressure. They won two Super Bowls with Roger Staubach and three with Troy Aikman. Despite his temporary sidelining as he recovers from his ankle injury, Dak is the undisputed leader of "America's Team" and that comes with a lot of pressure to perform. But the leadership he has shown on the field proves he will always have players on his side.

"Dak's willingness to be transparent and share his difficult times and share it with such stature, with class, you're just always going back to that word 'leadership,'" owner Jerry Jones said. "He is extremely gifted as a leader."[xxxvii]

Players and the organization have nothing but the utmost respect for a man who has been through so much in such a short time. They understand the adversity he has had to fight through in his personal life, how strong he has become, and how he has endured and powered through it. They also look up to how he selflessly helps others and the character and personality he displays off the field, always willing to help others and wanting to put smiles on faces.

Moving forward, Prescott will have to adjust to an ever-changing league, but one that clearly suits his style of play. The league has come down harder on defensive penalties and contact, allowing for quarterbacks to take greater advantage of one-on-one coverage and providing improved opportunities for deep-thrown balls. This suits Dak's ability to throw the ball deep, and with three potential Pro Bowl wide receivers in Cooper, Lamb, and Gallup, there is no doubt the Cowboys are eager to lock up the star quarterback to a long-term deal.

If 2020 was any indication up to the point of his injury, Prescott was getting better by the week. Once he returns to the field, defenses will no doubt have a hard time containing him. And if the Cowboys can just fix their defensive woes, they may make the playoffs and strap on for another Super Bowl run.

Conclusion

"I want to go where I'm the difference. I want to make something out of nothing. I want to be the reason someone is great."[iv] – Dak Prescott

It is a quote that best sums up Dak Prescott, a young man who has been a fighter all his life, wanting to make not just himself but also those around him better. He has worked hard for others, specifically his mother, to whom he dedicates each game whenever he steps on the field. He is not a selfish athlete, but rather one who is all about the team and making those around him the best possible athletes they can be.

Moving forward, Prescott will only get better, simply because he does not accept failure. He only accepts success and has a fierce determination to always be getting better. He wants to take the Cowboys to new heights and get them back to Super Bowl glory, just like they were under the leadership of Roger Staubach and Troy Aikman.

But no matter what Prescott the player turns into, Prescott the person is someone that every young athlete today can look up to. Dak is someone who gives back to the community and is all about a positive attitude. Someone who sets their goals high and works towards them, fighting through hardships along the way. Someone who cares about others and believes in them, knowing that he can make a positive difference in their lives. Someone who puts family first and will do whatever is necessary to make sure it is a priority in his life.

Dak Prescott is a role model for young people everywhere and someone we will all continue to root for every time he takes the field.

Final Word/About the Author

I was born and raised in Norwalk, Connecticut. Growing up, I could often be found spending many nights watching basketball, soccer, and football matches with my father in the family living room. I love sports and everything that sports can embody. I believe that sports are one of the most genuine forms of competition, heart, and determination. I write my works to learn more about influential athletes in the hopes that from my writing, you the reader can walk away inspired to put in an equal if not greater amount of hard work and perseverance to pursue your goals. If you enjoyed *Dak Prescott,* please leave a review! Also, you can read more of my works on *David Ortiz, Mike Trout, Bryce Harper, Jackie Robinson, Aaron Judge, Odell Beckham Jr., Bill Belichick, Serena Williams, Rafael Nadal, Roger Federer, Novak Djokovic, Richard Sherman, Andrew Luck, Rob Gronkowski, Brett Favre, Calvin Johnson, Drew Brees, J.J. Watt, Colin Kaepernick, Aaron Rodgers,*

Peyton Manning, Tom Brady, Russell Wilson, Odell Beckham Jr., Bill Belichick, Charles Barkley, Trae Young, Gregg Popovich, Pat Riley, John Wooden, Steve Kerr, Brad Stevens, Red Auerbach, Doc Rivers, Erik Spoelstra, Michael Jordan, LeBron James, Kyrie Irving, Klay Thompson, Stephen Curry, Kevin Durant, Russell Westbrook, Anthony Davis, Chris Paul, Blake Griffin, Kobe Bryant, Joakim Noah, Scottie Pippen, Carmelo Anthony, Kevin Love, Grant Hill, Tracy McGrady, Vince Carter, Patrick Ewing, Karl Malone, Tony Parker, Allen Iverson, Hakeem Olajuwon, Reggie Miller, Michael Carter-Williams, John Wall, James Harden, Tim Duncan, Steve Nash, Draymond Green, Kawhi Leonard, Dwyane Wade, Ray Allen, Pau Gasol, Dirk Nowitzki, Jimmy Butler, Paul Pierce, Manu Ginobili, Pete Maravich, Larry Bird, Kyle Lowry, Jason Kidd, David Robinson, LaMarcus Aldridge, Derrick Rose, Paul George, Kevin Garnett, Chris Paul, Marc Gasol, Yao Ming, Al Horford, Amar'e Stoudemire, DeMar DeRozan, Isaiah Thomas, Kemba

Walker, Chris Bosh, Andre Drummond, JJ Redick, DeMarcus Cousins, Wilt Chamberlain, Bradley Beal, Rudy Gobert, Aaron Gordon, Kristaps Porzingis, Nikola Vucevic, Andre Iguodala, Devin Booker, John Stockton, Jeremy Lin, Chris Paul, Pascal Siakam, Jayson Tatum, Gordon Hayward, Nikola Jokic, Bill Russell, Victor Oladipo, Luka Doncic, Ben Simmons, Shaquille O'Neal, Joel Embiid, Donovan Mitchell, Damian Lillard and *Giannis Antetokounmpo* in the Kindle Store. If you love football, check out my website at claytongeoffreys.com to join my exclusive list where I let you know about my latest books and give you lots of goodies.

Like what you read? Please leave a review!

I write because I love sharing the stories of influential athletes like Dak Prescott with fantastic readers like you. My readers inspire me to write more so please do not hesitate to let me know what you thought by leaving a review! If you love books on life, sports, or productivity, check out my website at claytongeoffreys.com to join my exclusive list where I let you know about my latest books. Aside from being the first to hear about my latest releases, you can also download a free copy of *33 Life Lessons: Success Principles, Career Advice & Habits of Successful People*. See you there!

Clayton

References

[i] "Dak Prescott Stats." Pro-Football Reference. Nd. Web.

[ii] "Dak Prescott Biography." *Thefamouspeople.com.* Nd. Web.

[iii] Sallee, Barrett. "Mississippi State HC Dan Mullen Talks Dak Prescott, Expectations and More." *The Bleacher Report.* 7 Apr 2014. Web.

[iv] "Dak Prescott Inspirational Quotes." *Brainy-Quote.* Nd. Web.

[v] Hill, Jr., Charles. "No Absentee: Dak Prescott's Father Has Always Been There." *The Star Telegram. 31* Jul 2017. Web.

[vi] Moore, David. "'She's the Reason That I Live Life': Why Every Day is Mother's Day for Cowboys QB Dak Prescott." *Dallas News.* 13 May 2018. Web.

[vii] Epstein, Jori. "Explore a Side of Dak Prescott You Haven't Seen Before Straight from his Childhood Friends." *Dallas News.* 1 Jul 2018. Web.

[viii] Fishman, Jon. "Sports All-Stars: Dak Prescott." *Lerner Publication.* 2019. Web.

[ix] Browning, William. "Dak Prescott's Hometown Beginnings." *The Columbus Dispatch.* 8 Oct 2014. Web.

[x] Thomas, Mike. "Dak Prescott Explains How an Insurance Job Shaped His Quarterback Career." *SportsCasting.com.* 18 Sep 2020. Web.

[xi] Prescott, Dak. "How Starkville Shaped Me: How Mississippi State's Role in Molding Me into the Quarterback and Man I am Today." *Sports Illustrated.* 23 Nov 2015.

[xii] "Dak Prescott College Stats." *Sports-Reference.* Nd. Web.

[xiii] "Mississippi State Athletics: Dak Prescott." *HailState.com.* Nd. Web.

[xiv] Coker, Reid. "Dak Prescott Lands Among Rare Company with 2014 Heisman Vote." *SB Nation.* 14 Dec 2014. Web.

[xv] Leigh, Brian. "Mississippi State QB Dak Prescott's Mother Passes Away.*" The Bleacher Report.* 4 Nov 2013. Web.

[xvi] Thomas, Mike. "Dak Prescott Remains a Mama's Boy Seven Years After His Mother's Death." *SporstCasting.com.* 15 Sep 2020. Web.

[xvii] Fitzgerald, Matt. "Dak Prescott, Mississippi State Teammates Attacked During Spring Break Concert." *The Bleacher Report.* 9 Mar 2015. Web.

[xviii] "2016 NFL Draft Scouting Report: Mississippi State QB Dak Prescott." *USA Today.* 24 Dec 2015. Web.

[xix] Glasspiegel, Ryan. "Most NFL Draft Pundits and All-NFL Teams Were Way Off on Dak Prescott." *The Big Lead.* 30 Nov 2016. Web.

[xx] "Cowboys Draft Dak Prescott, First QB Since 2009. *ESPN.* 30 Apr 2016. Web.

[xxi] Van Bibber, Ryan. "Dak Prescott Won the Cowboys QB Job, But it Didn't Happen Overnight." *SB Nation.* 17 Nov 2016. Web.

[xxii] Mays, Robert. "Dak Prescott is Having a Rookie Season for the Ages." *The Ringer.* 25 Nov 2016.

[xxiii] Lenix, Matthew. "Tony Romo Shares Insight on How he Handled Giving Prescott Keys to Cowboys." *USA Today.* 1 Apr 2020. Web.

[xxiv] Thamel, Pete. "Ahead of Schedule: Dak Prescott Exceeding All Expectations in Stellar Start to NFL Career." *Sports Illustrated.* 11 Oct 2016. Web.

[xxv] Archer, Todd. "Dak Prescott's 2017 Season Shows How Special He Was." *ESPN.* 26 Dec 2017. Web.

[xxvi] Modisette, Kevin. "Dak Prescott Owns Up to 2017 Struggles, Claims to Have the Fix.*" The USA Today.* 27 Jul 2018. Web.

[xxvii] Hill, Jr., Clarence. "Grown Man Dak Prescott and Cowboys are Moving on in the NFC Playoffs After 24-22 Win." *The Star Telegram.* 6 Jan 2019. Web.

[xxviii] Haislop, Todd. "Dak Prescott Contract Details: Why Cowboys QB is Playing Under Franchise Tag Without Long-Term Deal." *The Sporting News.* 14 Sep 2020. Web.

[xxix] Brito, Christopher. "Cowboys' Dak Prescott Reveals He Got Help for Depression." *CBS News.* 11 Sep 2020. Web.

[xxx] Nunez, Irwin. "Dak Prescott's is More Tragic Than You Think." *SportsCasting.* 17 Jul 2020. Web.

[xxxi] "Dak Prescott's Net Worth is Probably Higher than You Think." *SportsCasting.* 26 Jun 2020. Web.

[xxxii] Kapusta, Michelle. "Who is Dak Prescott's Girlfriend, Natalie Buffett?" *CheatSheet.com.* 20 Sep 2020. Web.

[xxxiii] Wilson, Ryan. "Dak Prescott Passed on Free Kanye West Tickets to Get Some Sleep." *CBS Sports.* 12 Oct 2016. Web.

xxxiv "10 Things You May Not Know About Cowboys QB Dak Prescott." Dallas News From Giving Up Kanye to His Adorable Dogs." *Dallas News.* 9 Feb 2019. Web.

xxxv Ochoa, R.J. "Dak Prescott made NFL history during his amazing performance in the Cowboys' comeback win." Blogging the Boys. 20 Sep 2020. Web.

xxxvi Lang III, Roy. "Dak at 50: Cowboys Quarterback Posts Historic Numbers Early in His Career." *The Shreveport Times.* 20 Sep 2019. Web.

xxxvii Phillips, Rob. "Jones: Dak is an 'Extremely Gifted Leader.'" *DallasCowboys.com.* 11 Sep 2020. Web.

xxxviii Hill, Jr., Clarence. "No Absentee: Dak Prescott's Father Has Always Been There." *The Star Telegram.* 17 Jul 2018. Web.

xxix "Dak Prescott: I Grew Up in a Trailer Park." *YouTube.* Uploaded 9 Sep 2020. Video.

xl "Dallas Cowboys with Chunky Soup: Dak Prescott Shares His Favorite Food Memory from Childhood. *Facebook.* Nd. Video.

xli "Dak Prescott: Mom Worried Government Would Take Kids." *YouTube.* Uploaded 9 Sep 2020. Video.

xlii Bonner, Matt. "Hometown Knew what Dak Prescott Could Do." *The Clarion Ledger.* 26 Oct 2014. Web.

xliii Williams, Charean. "Dak Prescott has compound fracture dislocation of his right ankle." *Profootballtalk.NBCSports.com.* 11 Oct 2020. Web.

Made in United States
North Haven, CT
21 May 2024

52795752R00076